People *of the* Alaskan Rain Forest

by Jacqueline Adams

Contents

Life in a Temperate Rain Forest

In the **temperate** rain forest of Alaska's southeast coast, cedar and spruce trees stand in the mist. Water silently drips from the tree branches. Mountains tower nearby, and bears fish for salmon in streams. The Native Alaskan Tlingit (KLINK it) have lived in this place of beauty for thousands of years.

Before explorers came to their land in 1741, the Tlingit got most of what they needed from the rain forest. They carved canoes, **totem poles,** and boxes from cedar wood. They wove baskets and rope from roots and bark.

▼ Many types of trees grow in the Alaskan rain forest, where the Tlingit have lived for thousands of years.

The Tlingit moved around to find food. In spring they fished and hunted otters and seals. In summer they moved to fishing camps near rivers to catch salmon. At hunting camps, they picked berries and hunted deer, bear, and mountain goats. They also took long canoe voyages to trade food and other goods in the summer.

Winter in a Tlingit Village

In wintertime the Tlingit settled in villages along rocky beaches, on islands, and in river valleys. About 12 families would live in a rectangular house usually made of cedar wood. To make more room inside, they dug out the dirt floor. Along the walls, they built low platforms for sitting and higher platforms for sleeping areas. They carved most of their wooden items here during the winter.

The Tlingit also hosted **potlatches** in their homes. During these great feasts, the Tlingit sang, danced, and showed their wealth by giving gifts. The feasts would last several days. There were potlatches for marriages, funerals, naming babies, and totem pole raisings. Guests helped set up the totem pole, and a speaker told stories about the figures carved on it.

But changes were coming that would soon threaten the Tlingit way of life.

Many materials used in Tlingit villages came from the dense Alaskan rain forests. ▶

3

Explorers Arrive in Alaska

In 1741 Russian explorers reached Alaska and claimed it for Russia, and fur traders soon arrived. In 1799 a group of Russian traders and Native Alaskan Aleut (ah LOOT) hunters came to Tlingit land and built a fort near the town of Sitka.

At first, the Tlingit traded with the newcomers. However, the Tlingit **resented** the Russian occupation of their land and control of their trade routes. The Tlingit attacked the fort several times in that first winter but did not manage to take over the fort.

In 1802 a Tlingit chief named Katlian led a huge attack on the fort. The Tlingit killed most of the Russians and Aleuts there. They burned the buildings and took back more than four thousand pelts from animals the Russians had hunted. The Tlingit felt the pelts rightfully belonged to them. Then they **fortified** an area near their village in case the Russians returned.

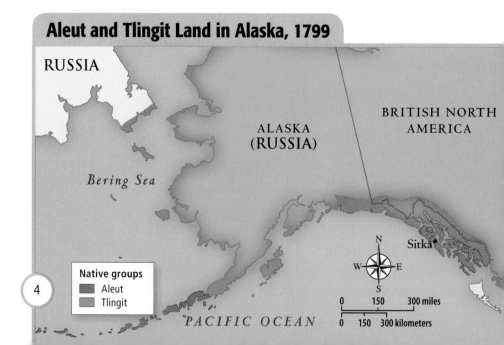

Aleut and Tlingit Land in Alaska, 1799

RUSSIA

ALASKA
(RUSSIA)

BRITISH NORTH
AMERICA

Bering Sea

Sitka

Native groups
- Aleut
- Tlingit

N
W—E
S

0   150   300 miles
0   150   300 kilometers

PACIFIC OCEAN

Trouble for the Tlingit

Two years later, four Russian ships carrying 1,150 Russians and Aleuts arrived. The Tlingit took refuge in their fort. For several days, the ships' cannons fired on them.

The Russians came ashore, but fierce fighting with the Tlingit forced the Russians back to their ships. They continued to fire the cannons until the Tlingit fled to the mountains. The Russians built a new settlement and fort at the site. For years afterward, Tlingit **warriors** continued to attack Russian settlements in Alaska.

Threats to the Tlingit multiplied. The newcomers had brought disease with them. Many Tlingit died from smallpox, influenza, and tuberculosis. Then Americans, who had traveled to Alaska in search of gold, took more Tlingit land. In 1867 Russia sold Alaska to the United States. The Tlingit, however, were not allowed to become American citizens.

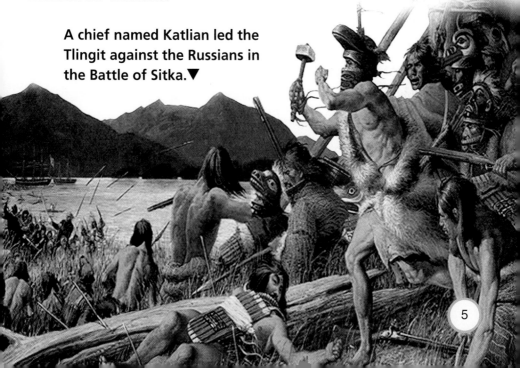

A chief named Katlian led the Tlingit against the Russians in the Battle of Sitka.▼

Fighting for Fair Treatment

In 1912 the Tlingit and other Native Alaskans formed the Alaska Native Brotherhood. The brotherhood fought for citizenship rights for Native Alaskan people, as well as the rights to vote and attend public school.

▲ Elizabeth Peratrovich fought for equal rights for Native Alaskans.

Even after Native Alaskans became citizens in 1924, businesses hung signs that read: "No Natives Allowed." The Tlingit suffered from **discrimination** at every turn. Then Tlingit leaders Roy and Elizabeth Peratrovich tried to rent a house. The owners refused to rent it to natives. In 1945 Elizabeth gave a speech to lawmakers and persuaded them to pass a law against native discrimination. Today, Alaskans celebrate Elizabeth Peratrovich Day every February 16 in remembrance of her struggle for their rights.

Later, in 1971, the United States passed the Alaska Native Claims Settlement Act. This law granted the Tlingit and nearby natives money and land in return for the land that had been taken from them.

Keeping Traditions Alive

Today, most of the Tlingit live their day-to-day lives in modern houses and in modern clothing. But they still observe the traditions of their ancestors. They hold potlatches, wear special ceremonial clothing, and make the traditional crafts of their ancestors.

Tlingit artists today continue to carve and weave as their ancestors did. They also make special traditional crafts. One of the most well known, the Chilkat blanket, takes about one year to weave. These blankets are made of mountain goat wool and cedar bark fiber. Chilkat blankets are traditionally a sign of wealth, and they are worn as robes.

Tlingit history has involved great struggles for freedom and for rights, but the people are true to their heritage. Although the world has changed around them, the Tlingit culture is alive and thriving.

▼ Tlingit family signs are woven into Chilkat blankets, which are worn as robes during ceremonies.

Glossary

discrimination unfair treatment of a certain group

fortified strengthened against attack

potlatches Native American feasts at which many gifts are given

resented disliked; were angered by

temperate mild in temperature, without extremes of hot and cold

totem poles animals and other images carved into huge tree trunks that tell about Tlingit families' histories and stories

warriors great fighters

Activities

Check Understanding

1. **Recall** How did Elizabeth Peratrovich help the Tlingit?

2. **Analyze** Why might outsiders like the Russians have wanted Tlingit land?

3. **Reader Response** Would you like to have lived in a Tlingit village thousands of years ago? Why or why not?

Reading Skill

Compare and Contrast Think about Tlingit life today and long ago. How are these two ways of life alike? How are they different?

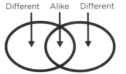

Writing in Social Studies

Diary You live in a Tlingit village in the 1600s. It is summertime. How do you spend your day? Write about it in your diary.

SOCIAL STUDIES
Leveled
Reader
Library

The **McGraw·Hill** Companies

ISBN: 978-0-02-152054-1
MHID: 0-02-152054-2

Mc
Graw
Hill

Macmillan/McGraw-Hill
Glencoe

KARATE
TRAINING
GUIDE

VOLUME 2

KATA—HEIAN, TEKKI, BASSAI DAI

RANDALL G. HASSELL